TELL THE

BY ABBY BADACH

# THE TALE OF
# RIP VAN WINKLE

Enslow
PUBLISHING

INVESTIGATE!

Please visit our website, www.enslow.com. For a free color catalog of all our high-quality books, call toll free 1-800-398-2504 or fax 1-877-980-4454.

**Library of Congress Cataloging-in-Publication Data**

Names: Doyle, Abby Badach, author.
Title: The tale of Rip Van Winkle / Abby Badach Doyle.
Description: Buffalo, New York : Enslow Publishing, [2024] | Series: Tell
  the tale | Includes index. | Audience:
  Grades 2-3
Identifiers: LCCN 2023008321 (print) | LCCN 2023008322 (ebook) | ISBN
  9781978535435 (library binding) | ISBN 9781978535428 (paperback) | ISBN
  9781978535442 (ebook)
Subjects: LCSH: Irving, Washington, 1783-1859. Rip Van Winkle–Juvenile
  literature. | Van Winkle, Rip (Fictitious character)–Juvenile
  literature.
Classification: LCC PS2068 .D69 2024  (print) | LCC PS2068  (ebook) | DDC
  813/.2–dc23/eng/20230302
LC record available at https://lccn.loc.gov/2023008321
LC ebook record available at https://lccn.loc.gov/2023008322

Portions of this work were originally authored by Mark Harasymiw and published as *The Legend of Rip Van Winkle*. All new material in this edition is authored by Abby Badach Doyle.

Published in 2024 by
**Enslow Publishing**
2544 Clinton Street
Buffalo, NY 14224

Copyright © 2024 Enslow Publishing

Designer: Tanya Dellaccio Keeney and Claire Wrazin
Editor: Abby Badach Doyle

Photo credits: Series art (leather background) Rawpixel.com/Shutterstock.com, (paper background) Daboost/Shutterstock.com, (metal plate) maxstockphoto/Shutterstock.com, (explore more background) Didecs/Shutterstock.com; cover, p. 1 (Rip Van Winkle) NotionPic/Shutterstock.com; cover, p. 1 (background) NEILRAS/Shutterstock.com; p. 5 File:Rip_Van_Winkle's_return_-_Gillam._LCCN2012645456.jpg/Wikimedia Commons; p. 7 (map) EmLion/Shutterstock.com; p. 9 File:Rip_Van_Winkle-053.jpg/Wikimedia Commons; p. 11 File:Joseph_Jefferson_as_Rip_Van_Winkle_in_"Rip_Van_Winkle"_-_DPLA_-_6ae670041b2a108d0cbe039ce2b5e946.jpg/Wikimedia Commons; p. 13 File:Washington_Irving_Rip_Van_Winkle_1888_illustrator_Frank_T_Merrill_A_company_of_odd-looking_personages.jpg/Wikimedia Commons; p. 15 File:Henry_Inman_-_Rip_Van_Winkle_Awakening_from_his_Long_Sleep_-_2018.44.134_-_National_Gallery_of_Art.jpg/Wikimedia Commons; p. 17 File:Joseph_Jefferson_as_Rip_Van_Winkle_in_"Rip_Van_Winkle"_-_DPLA_-_6d9f421d914403923c1bdb1f59b585df.jpg/Wikimedia Commons; p. 19 File:Rip_Van_Winkle-109.jpg/Wikimedia Commons; p. 21 File:King_George_III_of_England_by_Johann_Zoffany.jpg/Wikimedia Commons; p. 23 File:Rip_Van_Winkle-125.jpg/Wikimedia Commons; p. 25 File:Fritz_Freund_-_Ziegenhirte_auf_der_Alm.jpg/Wikimedia Commons; p. 27 (arrow) ildogesto/Shutterstock.com; p. 27 (portrait of Irving) File:Washington_Irving_at_22.jpg/Wikimedia Commons; p. 29 Kenneth Sponsler/Shutterstock.com.

Printed in the United States of America

CPSIA compliance information: Batch #CSENS24: For further information contact Enslow Publishing at 1-800-398-2504.

Find us on

# CONTENTS

One Foggy Morning . . . . . . . . . . . . . . . . . . . . . 4

Meet Rip Van Winkle. . . . . . . . . . . . . . . . . . . . 6

A Messy Home . . . . . . . . . . . . . . . . . . . . . . . . 8

No Ordinary Hike. . . . . . . . . . . . . . . . . . . . . 10

Getting Sleepy . . . . . . . . . . . . . . . . . . . . . . . 12

Good Morning! . . . . . . . . . . . . . . . . . . . . . . . 14

Leaving the Woods . . . . . . . . . . . . . . . . . . . . 16

To the Village . . . . . . . . . . . . . . . . . . . . . . . . 18

Who's In Charge?. . . . . . . . . . . . . . . . . . . . . 20

A Familiar Face . . . . . . . . . . . . . . . . . . . . . . 22

An Old German Tale . . . . . . . . . . . . . . . . . . 24

The American Voice . . . . . . . . . . . . . . . . . . . 26

Taking a Chance. . . . . . . . . . . . . . . . . . . . . . 28

Glossary . . . . . . . . . . . . . . . . . . . . . . . . . . . 30

For More Information. . . . . . . . . . . . . . . . . . 31

Index. . . . . . . . . . . . . . . . . . . . . . . . . . . . . . 32

Words in the glossary appear in **bold** type the first time they are used in the text.

# ONE FOGGY MORNING

Imagine you are so tired you must lie down and take a nap. When you finally wake up, you realize you've been asleep for 20 years! That's what happens to Rip Van Winkle, the main character in a famous tale by Washington Irving.

When Rip Van Winkle falls asleep, New York is still one of the 13 British colonies. People obey the rules set by King George III. Rip Van Winkle wakes up to a place that feels very different. Later, he finds out he slept through the **American Revolution**!

## EXPLORE MORE!

*Washington Irving was born in New York City in 1783. The same year, the American Revolution ended. His parents named him after George Washington. As a boy, Washington Irving saw George Washington take the oath, or promise, to serve as president.*

The short story "Rip Van Winkle" was published in 1819.

# MEET RIP VAN WINKLE

Rip Van Winkle is a kind, fun-loving man. He plays games and tells stories with the children in his village. He loves taking long walks in the beautiful Catskill Mountains. He likes hunting and fishing. The village wives enjoy his company. They ask for his help with small tasks. He never refuses to help a neighbor, even with very hard work.

However, Rip finds it impossible to do his own work. He just doesn't enjoy tending to his farm or making money for himself. So, Rip and his family are quite poor.

## EXPLORE MORE!

*The short story "Rip Van Winkle" was said to have taken place in the Catskill Mountains and the Hudson River valley. These are real places in New York State. In the story, the name is spelled as "Kaatskill Mountains."*

# WHERE ARE THE CATSKILL MOUNTAINS?

NEW YORK

Hudson River

ALBANY

Catskill
Mountains

Hudson
Valley

NEW YORK CITY

The Catskills are located between Albany
and New York City.

# A MESSY HOME

With no one tending to it, the Van Winkle farm is a mess. The fences are falling apart. Weeds grow everywhere. Even the cow wanders off. It steps on the cabbages they planted.

Rip doesn't mind that his children dress in clothes that are worn-out. He likes his simple life and doesn't see the need to change. However, his wife Dame Van Winkle sees things differently. She can't stand her husband's **lazy** ways! She nags him morning, noon, and night. When she yells at Rip, he just walks away.

## EXPLORE MORE!

*Rip has a faithful dog named Wolf. Dame Van Winkle doesn't like Wolf. She thinks he makes her husband even more lazy. Wolf is afraid of Dame Van Winkle and her yelling! His tail sinks down when he sees her in the house.*

**Nag means to annoy someone with repeat orders.**

# NO ORDINARY HIKE

On a beautiful autumn day, Rip and Wolf go squirrel hunting. Rip needs some peace and quiet from Dame Van Winkle! After walking a while, he sits down to rest. While he is sitting, he hears his name being called. "Rip Van Winkle! Rip Van Winkle!" Wolf begins to growl.

Rip sees a man carrying a heavy barrel on his back. He is dressed in old-fashioned Dutch clothing. "Dutch" is the name given to the people of the Netherlands, a European country. He motions to Rip to ask for help.

## EXPLORE MORE!

*Dutch settlers came to America in the early 1600s. They named their settlement New Amsterdam. Amsterdam is the capital city of the Netherlands. In 1664, the English took over the area. They renamed it New York, which is what we call it today.*

A barrel holds liquids. It is made of wood with round sides and flat ends.

# GETTING SLEEPY

It is strange to see another person this far back in the woods. Rip doesn't know the man, so he **hesitates** to approach him. But Rip wants to help, so he joins the stranger. Together, they walk a long way up through the mountains.

Then they come across a group of men. These men are also dressed in strange, old-fashioned clothing. They are playing ninepins, a bowling game! It makes a noise like thunder. After a while, Rip helps himself to the strong drink from the barrel. Soon, he falls asleep.

## EXPLORE MORE!

In his story, Washington Irving describes the strange men in great **detail**. One has a large head with "small piggish eyes." Another has a nose almost as big as his face! All the men have different color beards. Some wear silly hats.

As time passes, Rip knows he'll be home
long after dark!

# GOOD MORNING!

Rip wakes up to a bright, sunny morning. He is in a different spot than the clearing where he had fallen asleep. That is strange! He must have slept through the night. He knows he has to get home. Dame Van Winkle will be angry.

Rip looks around for his gun, but he can't find it. The only gun he finds is old and covered in rust. Rip always keeps his gun clean. That rusty gun couldn't be his. He wonders if the strange men stole it while he slept.

## EXPLORE MORE!

*Iron is a type of metal. Over time, it turns to rust. This happens when iron **reacts** with water and oxygen, a gas in the air. Can you guess why Rip found a rusty gun instead of his clean one?*

Rip knows he had slept much longer than he meant to.

# LEAVING THE WOODS

Rip calls for his dog, but Wolf doesn't come. He must be lost in the forest, Rip thinks. Maybe he ran after a squirrel. Or maybe the strange men took Wolf too! Rip doesn't want to wait for Wolf. He stands up to walk, but it hurts. He slowly hikes down the mountain.

Rip is worried to meet his angry wife. But first, there is a more important problem. He is getting hungry! He knows he won't find a good breakfast in the mountains. So, Rip walks down to the village.

## EXPLORE MORE!

*The Catskill Mountains have beautiful hiking trails. Today, you can hike to a place called Rip's Rock. It is said to look like the place where Rip took his nap. From the top, there is great view of the Hudson Valley.*

As Rip walks, he notices the forest had grown wild.

# TO THE VILLAGE

When Rip gets to the village, things feel weird. More people live there, but he doesn't recognize anyone he knows. Everyone is dressed in strange fashions. People give him curious looks. They stroke their chins, so Rip does the same. To his amazement, he finds his beard is about 1 foot (30 cm) long!

That isn't all that has changed. Rip's house has fallen apart, so he goes to the village inn. It has a new name—The Union Hotel, by Jonathan Doolittle. Out front, he sees a new flag with stars and stripes.

## EXPLORE MORE!

*The United States of America named its official flag on June 14, 1777. Before that, each colony flew its own flag. The official flag, called the Stars and Stripes, stands for **unity**. Today's flag still has 13 stripes for the original 13 colonies.*

The village children point and laugh at
Rip's huge beard.

# WHO'S IN CHARGE?

The inn always had a picture of King George III wearing a red coat. But even this had changed! Now, it is a different man wearing a blue coat. It says, "General Washington."

Everyone there wants to talk about the government. People ask who Rip is. Rip says, "I am a poor, quiet man, a native of the place, and a **loyal** subject of the King, God bless him!" The people grow angry. Rip says he means no harm. He just wants to see his friends. Where have they gone?

## EXPLORE MORE!

*The townspeople call Rip a Tory and a* **spy**. *During the American Revolution, a Tory was a person still in favor of British rule. People who supported American independence called themselves patriots. A patriot is a person who loves their country.*

King George III ruled Great Britain and Ireland from 1760–1820.

# A FAMILIAR FACE

Finally, Rip learns why everyone is acting so funny. It turns out that 20 years have passed while he was asleep! A woman recognizes him and explains everything. She is Rip's daughter, Judith.

In the time that has passed, Judith has married and named a son after him. Dame Van Winkle has died. Rip's son has grown to have habits like his father. Rip moves in with Judith. He enjoys the rest of his life, taking walks and telling stories. He tells many people his own story of that walk in the woods!

## EXPLORE MORE!

*An old man told Rip he knew the strangely dressed man from the woods. He said it was Henry Hudson! He was an early European explorer of that area. Hudson and his men haunted the Catskills every 20 years.*

Now an old man, Rip enjoys life without having to work.

# AN OLD GERMAN TALE

In 1818, Washington Irving had the idea to write the story "Rip Van Winkle." But he didn't come up with the idea all on his own. He based it on an old German story, "Peter Klaus the Goatherd." In this tale, Peter's goats begin to go missing. One by one, they walk through a hole in the wall.

Peter follows them. He finds German knights playing ninepins on the other side. He has a strong drink and falls asleep. Peter also awoke 20 years later. He lived happily ever after.

## EXPLORE MORE!

*Washington Irving changed some details in the story. He wrote Rip to be more likeable than Peter. And of course, "Rip Van Winkle" is set in New York instead of Germany. The bowling men are Dutch settlers, not knights.*

A goatherd is a person who takes care of a group of goats.

# THE AMERICAN VOICE

Washington Irving was one of the most famous writers in the 1800s. He is most remembered for writing short stories such as "Rip Van Winkle" and "The Legend of Sleepy Hollow." These were published in a collection called *The Sketch Book of Geoffrey Crayon*. Sometimes, he wrote using the name Geoffrey Crayon or Jonathan Oldstyle.

Washington Irving also wrote newspaper articles, poems, and books. Many of them were funny. Other writings were serious. Some of his best-known books were **biographies** of important leaders, such as George Washington and Christopher Columbus.

## EXPLORE MORE!

*While Washington Irving was alive, the United States was still a young nation. Many Europeans didn't know what it was like to live there. Through his writing, Washington Irving told stories of American people and places. The stories were rich with detail and wit.*

# WASHINGTON IRVING'S LIFE

**1832**
moves back to
United States

**1826–32**
travels to Spain

**1842–46**
works for the U.S.
government in Spain

**APRIL 3, 1783**
born in New York City

**1815**
moves to England
and starts writing as
"Geoffrey Crayon"

**1855–59**
publishes biography of
George Washington

**1819–20**
publishes "Rip Van
Winkle" and "The
Legend of Sleepy
Hollow"

**NOVEMBER 28, 1859**
dies at his home in
Tarrytown, New York

Washington Irving spent his life writing and traveling between Europe and the United States.

# TAKING A CHANCE

As a child, Washington Irving loved to read, write, and draw. When he grew up, he worked as a **lawyer**. Quickly, he realized he didn't like it! So, he took a chance and started writing more instead. Now, we can see that chance paid off.

Washington Irving helped other writers too. He saw the harm that happened when someone would copy a writer's work. He suggested stronger laws to make that a crime. More than 200 years later, Washington Irving is still remembered as one of the great American writers.

## EXPLORE MORE!

*Today, you can tour Washington Irving's home in Tarrytown, New York. He named it "Sunnyside." It sits on the banks of the Hudson River and has beautiful gardens. He gathered there with other writers, as well as artists and government leaders.*

**Washington Irving bought his famous stone home in 1835.**

# GLOSSARY

**American Revolution:** The war in which the colonies won their freedom from England.

**biography:** A story of a real person's life written by someone other than that person.

**detail:** A small part of something.

**hesitate:** To stop briefly before you are about to do something.

**lawyer:** Someone whose job it is to help people with their questions and problems with the law.

**lazy:** Not liking to work hard or be active.

**loyal:** Faithful.

**publish:** To have something you wrote included in a book, magazine, or newspaper.

**react:** To change after coming in contact with another substance.

**spy:** A person who secretly tries to get information about a country to support another.

**unity:** The state of being in full agreement.

# FOR MORE INFORMATION

## BOOKS

Irving, Washington. *Rip Van Winkle and The Legend of Sleepy Hollow*. Scottsdale, AZ: EDCON Publishing Group, 2020.

Irving, Washington, and Gemma Bardner. *Rip Van Winkle*. Leicester, England: Sweet Cherry Publishing, 2022.

Krull, Kathleen. *A Kids' Guide to the American Revolution*. New York, NY: Harper, 2018.

## WEBSITES

**Britannica Kids: Washington Irving**
kids.britannica.com/kids/article/Washington-Irving/353305
Read a history of Washington Irving's life and work.

**DK Find Out! American Revolution**
dkfindout.com/us/history/american-revolution
Learn facts and see pictures from the time period of the "Rip Van Winkle" story.

**Kiddle: Catskill Mountain Facts for Kids**
kids.kiddle.co/Catskill_Mountains
See photos of the area where the "Rip Van Winkle" story took place.

**Publisher's note to educators and parents:** Our editors have carefully reviewed these websites to ensure that they are suitable for students. Many websites change frequently, however, and we cannot guarantee that a site's future contents will continue to meet our high standards of quality and educational value. Be advised that students should be closely supervised whenever they access the internet.

# INDEX

American Revolution, 4, 20

Catskill Mountains, 6, 7, 16, 22

colonies, 4, 18

Columbus, Christopher, 26

Crayon, Geoffrey, 26, 27

Dame Van Winkle, 8, 10, 14, 16, 22

Dutch, 10, 24

Hudson, Henry, 22

Hudson River valley, 6, 7, 16, 28

Irving, Washington, 4, 12, 24, 26, 27, 28, 29

King George III, 4, 20, 21

"Legend of Sleepy Hollow, The," 26, 27

New York, 4, 6, 7, 10, 24, 28

New York City, 4, 7, 27

Oldstyle, Jonathan, 26

"Peter Klaus the Goatherd," 24

*Sketchbook of Geoffrey Crayon, The,* 26

Sunnyside, 28, 29

Tarrytown, New York, 27, 28

Washington, George, 4, 26, 27

Wolf, 8, 10, 16